ISBN 978-1-5276-3666-8
PIBN 10877193

1 MONTH OF
FREE
READING

at

www.ForgottenBooks.com

By purchasing this book you are eligible for one month membership to ForgottenBooks.com, giving you unlimited access to our entire collection of over 1,000,000 titles via our web site and mobile apps.

To claim your free month visit:

www.forgottenbooks.com/free877193

English
Français
Deutsche
Italiano
Español
Português

www.forgottenbooks.com

Mythology Photography **Fiction**
Fishing Christianity **Art** Cooking
Essays Buddhism Freemasonry
Medicine **Biology** Music **Ancient**
Egypt Evolution Carpentry Physics
Dance Geology **Mathematics** Fitness
Shakespeare **Folklore** Yoga Marketing
Confidence Immortality Biographies
Poetry **Psychology** Witchcraft
Electronics Chemistry History **Law**
Accounting **Philosophy** Anthropology
Alchemy Drama Quantum Mechanics
Atheism Sexual Health **Ancient History**
Entrepreneurship Languages Sport
Paleontology Needlework Islam
Metaphysics Investment Archaeology
Parenting Statistics Criminology
Motivational

UNIVERSITY OF CALIFORNIA

COLLEGE OF AGRICULTURE

BERKELEY

AGRICULTURAL EXPERIMENT STATION

BENJ. IDE WHEELER, President
THOMAS FORSYTH HUNT, Dean and Director
H. E. VAN NORMAN, Vice-Director and Dean
University Farm School

CIRCULAR No. 142.

November, 1915.

PRACTICAL AND INEXPENSIVE POULTRY APPLIANCES.

By J. E. DOUGHERTY and W. E. LLOYD.

The following pages describe and illustrate a number of practical, labor-saving and inexpensive poultry appliances, that have either been designed or improved by the Poultry Division of the College of. Agriculture, University of California. The primary aim in designing or improving these appliances has been (1) to make them as low in cost as possible so that expense of this nature might be kept low, (2) to make the designs very simple so that any one with ordinary skill in handling a hammer and saw could readily make them at home, (3) to produce appliances that would work, and work efficiently.

TRAPNESTS.

Poultrymen are coming to realize more fully, year by year, the great value of the trapnest in breeding for egg production, just as dairymen have come to appreciate the enormous value of the scales and Babcock tester in improving a dairy herd. In order to know accurately just how many eggs a hen produces; in order to know which are the boarders and which are the profitable fowls, trapnests must be used. The purpose of a trapnest is *not to* increase the egg production of the present layers but to find out just how well the best of the present flock are laying, in order that the good layers may be identified and mated to males out of good layers, for use as breeding stock to reproduce offspring with better laying qualities than the average of the present flock. Trapnest the *breeders* for they are going to produce the future layers, but do not *force* them for egg production. The hen that *naturally* produces better than her sisters is more prolific and will make the best breeder. The ideal average egg production may be fixed at 180 eggs per hen per year, which is considerably above the average production of commercial flocks of 500 or more hens. The present average may be raised towards this ideal by breeding from *naturally*

19325

strong layers, year after year, that lay well-shaped, nicely **colored**, good sized (2 ounces), strong-shelled eggs; that have good type and abundant vigor, and by mating them to well-grown, sturdy males out of naturally prolific mothers.

California Trapnest No. 1.—This is a simple box nest costing very little more to build than an ordinary wooden nest. The trapdoor is hinged at the top. To set nest the door is swung inward and held at the bottom by a wire hook (see figure 1) at JUST THE RIGHT HEIGHT SO THAT WHEN A HEN ENTERS THE NEST AND WALKS UNDER THE DOOR, HER BACK WILL RAISE IT UP just enough to release the hook and allow the door to swing quietly shut behind her. The door does not close with a bang but slips slowly down the fowl's back and over her tail after the hook is released and as the hen goes farther into the nest.

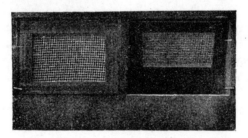

FIG. 1. California Trapnest No. 1 (modified Connecticut Trapnest). The end views above show how the trapdoor is set and how the inside stop locks the door from the inside after it is tripped.

As the door swings shut against the outside door stop (a 3-inch straight screw hook), the inside door stop (a bent piece of No. 6 wire) drops down (see figure 1a) and locks it from the inside.

To release the hen, turn the outside door stop up, swing the door outward and catch her in the two extended hands as she comes out. Then tuck her under the left arm, slide the left hand under her breast and seize the shanks at the hock joints. Hold the shanks up, read and note the legband which should be placed with the figures upside down on the fowl's leg so that it may be easily read when the fowl is held as here described and then let her go. When saving eggs for hatching the hen number, pen number and date are usually marked on the large end of the egg thus 268/27/2-10, after releasing the hen. At other

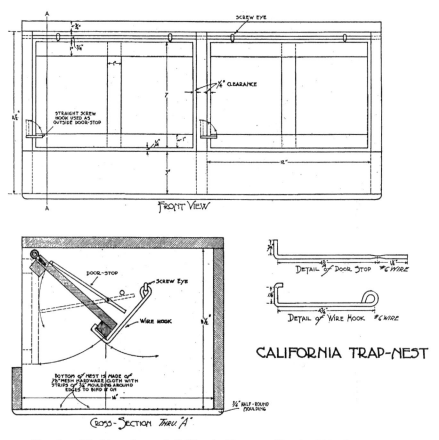

FIG. 1a. Working plans of California Trapnest No. 1. This drawing shows a wooden door as shown in Fig. 4 instead of the wire door illustrated in Fig. 1. Either style may be used. Bottom of trap door is hung 5¾ inches above bottom of nest when set for Leghorns and other small breeds. For the larger breeds, it will have to be set higher.

times the egg is simply credited to the hen on the record sheet hanging in the pen. A blank form of record sheet may be secured on application to the Poultry Division of the University of California.

To reset the nest, insert a pencil between the door and the side of the nest raising the inside stop with the left hand; push the door inward with the right hand and hook it in place. Then turn the outside door stop back to a horizontal position. Both the hook and inside door stop should be on the left side of nest to facilitate of setting nest quickly.

California Trapnest No. 2.—This trapnest is similar to the No. 1 nest, except that with trapnest No. 1 a 6- or 8-inch platform must be placed in front of the nest for the hen to jump upon in order to get into the nest (see figure 3), whereas with trapnest No. 2 this platform is made a part of the nest thus making it deeper from front to rear. As a result of uniting the front platform and nest into one nest and moving the trap door forward to the front edge of the platform, no

Fig. 2. California Trapnest No. 2.

inside stop is needed and the nest is simplified. It takes somewhat less time to run this style of trapnest and release the layers where there are no inside stops to raise when resetting the nest each time, whereas the cost of construction is slightly higher. Further, in operating No. 2 nest, the outside stop need never be turned. The necessary turning of the outside stop of nest No. 1 when releasing a hen wears the screw hole larger after a time and it has to be plugged. However, this is a small matter that five minutes' occasional attention will take care of.

The operation of the nest is exactly the same as that of the No. 1 nest except in releasing the layer. To release her after she has laid, push the trapdoor inward and upward above the hen's head and catch her in the extended hands as she comes out under the trapdoor, just as described above for the No. 1 nest.

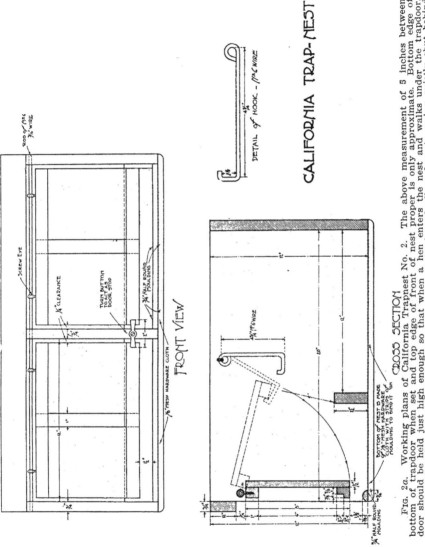

FIG. 2a. Working plans of California Trapnest No. 2. The above measurement of 5 inches between bottom of trapdoor when set and top edge of front of nest proper is only approximate. Bottom edge of door should be held just high enough so that when a hen enters the nest and walks under the trapdoor, her back will raise it up just high enough to release hook and allow door to swing quietly shut behind her. Bottom cleat of trapdoor may be made with a notch to catch hook as shown here or it may be left plain as shown in Fig. 1a.

To reset, push the trapdoor inward and fasten in position with the wire hook as shown in figure 2 and 2a.

The No. 1 style trapnest may be built in tiers against the wall as shown in figure 3, or they may be built under the droppings boards.

FIG. 3. No. 1 trapnests in a double tier against the wall of the pen. Note platforms in front of each nest.

The No. 2 style is best suited for use under the droppings boards or on the wall where nests are not tiered. The No. 2 nest can not be placed in tiers because the hen must jump directly into the nest from the floor. There can be no platform board placed in front of the nests for fowls to light on before entering to lay, as is done with the No. 1 nest, because no inside stops are used.

The reader will notice in the illustrations different styles of trapdoors used. We have experimented with a number of different styles of door in designing these nests and find that the solid door with plain cleats at the top and bottom, as shown in figure 2, to quickly catch the wire hook. and a 1-inch wide opening in the middle (see figure 2) is easiest to make, keeps the nest dark, yet permits of good ventilation, and the center opening enables the operator to readily see into the nest.* The wire door is a good one but lets more light into the nest. The bottoms of these

---

*The center opening in trapdoor should be only 1 inch wide so the hen can not put her head through while waiting to be released.

nests are made of ⅛-inch mesh hardware cloth. This permits all dirt and soiled nesting material to sift through as it is broken up and keeps the nest much more clean with less labor.

FIG. 4. No. 2 trapnests under the droppings board. Note the absence of any platform boards in front of nests for hens to jump on before entering. Instead they jump directly into front part of nest.

HOPPERS.

Dry Mash Hopper.—The dry mash hopper shown in figures 5 and 6 is positive in action because (unlike self-feeding hoppers) it can not clog. Self-feeding mash hoppers invariably either clog up or feed so fast that a great deal is scattered on the floor and wasted. This hopper is non-wasting if not filled too full because the ¾-inch wire mesh grid, which is simply a piece of ¾-inch mesh hardware cloth, prevents the fowls from hooking the feed out. It will hold a week's supply of mash for 35 fowls when made 2 feet long as shown in figure 5a. It may be made any length desired.

The Hopper should be placed on a feeding platform 15 inches off the floor so that the hens can not scratch it full of litter.

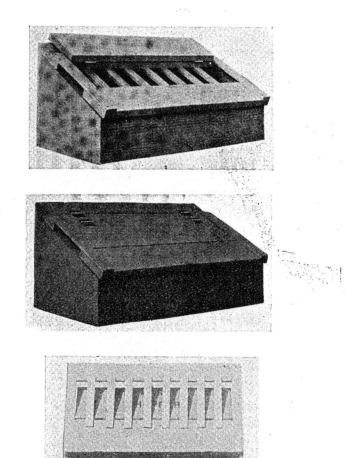

FIG. 5. California Dry Mash Hopper. The piece of ¾-inch mesh hardware cloth is laid on the feed to prevent the fowls hooking the mash out and wasting it.

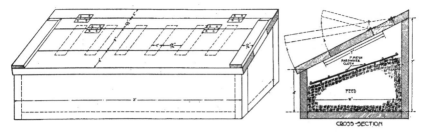

CALIFORNIA DRY MASH HOPPER

FIG. 5a. Working plans of California Dry Mash Hopper.

FIG. 6. Showing dry mash hoppers in use. Observe 15-inch high platform to keep hoppers up off ground where they will not be scratched full of dirt and litter.

Grit or Shell Hopper.—This is a simple self-feeding hopper with a wooden lip on the front edge of the opening where the fowls feed to prevent them from hooking the grit or shell out on the floor (see figures 7 and 7a). This style of hopper works very well with shell and grit because they feed easily and do not clog in the upper part of the hopper so readily as ground mill feeds. The grit will always feed well in this style of hopper but if the oyster shell used is rather fine, it may clog slightly in the narrow part of the throat of the feeder. If the attendant will look at the hoppers occasionally as he passes through each pen no trouble will be experienced. Properly constructed, this is one of the simplest and most satisfactory grit or shell hoppers that can be used.

FIG. 7. Grit or shell hopper.

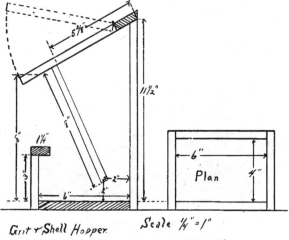

Grit r Shell Hopper.   Scale ¼"=1"

FIG. 7a. Working plans of grit or shell hopper.

Chick Mash Hopper.—The chick mash hopper shown in figure 8 is extremely simple and answers the purpose in every way. It consists merely of a shallow box or tray in which the grain or dry mash mixture is placed. The ½-inch mesh hardware cloth which is cut ⅛-inch smaller all around than the inside dimensions of the bottom of tray, is laid on top of the feed so as to prevent the chicks from scratching the feed out on the ground, yet they can get all the feed in the tray as they want it by picking through the hardware cloth. Care should be taken not to leave the edges of the hardware cloth too rough or they will scratch the chick's

FIG. 8. Chick Mash Hopper. A hopper 2 feet long, 5 inches wide and 1½ inches high, inside dimensions, is a very convenient size.

feet. The edges might be bound with a narrow edging of galvanized iron at but little extra expense. Only as much grain or dry mash should be put into the trays each day as will be consumed that day. Then each night they can be scraped out clean with a shingle or a fifteen-cent scraper ready for use the next day. These trays are being used at the Experiment Station for all chicks from the time they leave the incubator until they are half grown and able to use the large mash hoppers. If it is desired, they may be made wider for the older chicks, but the size shown is very satisfactory and easily handled.

FIG. 9. Catching Hook (after Cornell).

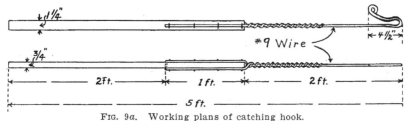

FIG. 9a. Working plans of catching hook.

Catching Hook.—In figures 9 and 9a are shown a catching hook which is very convenient, when properly handled, in catching up birds that the attendant desires to examine or remove from the pen. It is as a rule very difficult to get close enough to a fowl, especially one of the more active and nervous breeds, to pick her up with one's hands. It generally happens that when one really wants to catch a certain fowl, she simply won't let one get within arm's length. With the catching hook, one can slip up close enough with much less wear and tear on both attendant and fowl. Care must be exercised not to have the hook too tightly closed or to jerk the fowl too suddenly when catching her for when the hook is thus carelessly used, there is danger of bruising the skin of the shanks or even breaking a leg. Where used with normal care this hook is almost indispensable around the poultry yards. One should be kept hanging on a nail in each pen where it is quickly available in catching sick fowls as soon as discovered or other birds that it may be desirable to move from the pen.

The Catching Coop.—This coop is a very convenient device to use when treating fowls for body lice, for sorting or for transferring pens of chickens from pen to pen or from one house to another or whenever it is necessary to catch chickens in large numbers. When it is desired to

FIG. 10. Catching Coop.

FIG. 10a.

sort over a pen of fowls, the front end of the coop is pushed tightly against the chick exit, a coop full of chickens run in and the front sliding door closed. The coop may be then loaded on to a wagon or carried to the place where the sorting is to be done. The fowls are taken out one by one through the top doors, examined individually and

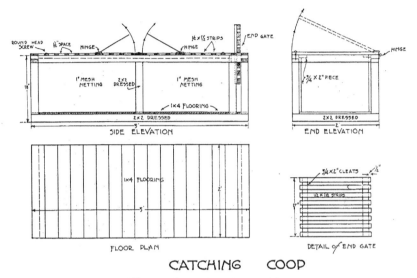

CATCHING COOP

FIG. 10b. Working plans for catching coop.

distributed as desired. Pens of chicks are quickly transferred from brooders to colony houses or easily sorted by its use. Such a coop must be light in weight, convenient to handle and covered with netting for ventilation so that the fowls will not smother. Rope handles may be fastened on each end for convenience in carrying. The top of the coop is hinged so that it can be raised and the coop easily cleaned when needed.

A Blood Can for Use in Killing and Picking.—Killing fowls by ''sticking'' them through the mouth is the usual way of killing for market because the bird is not only well bled but the head is left on so that the buyer can tell the sex as well as gain other valuable points indicated by the head to those who know fowls. In dry picking it is necessary to kill in this way to loosen the feathers. When using this method of killing the fowl is hung up by the feet with the breast toward the operator. A simple way of suspending a fowl is to hang a stout cord with a cork or circular block of wood ¾-inch thick by 1-inch wide fastened to the free end, from a beam just above the operator's head.

The fowl is then held head downward with both feet together and the cord twisted around the shanks and caught with the block of wood. The fowl's head is held in the left hand and the "stick" made with the right, after which a blood can (see figure 11) is hooked into the fleshy part of the lower mandible from the outside. This can should possess a sharp hook, be of proper diameter so that there is room to easily hook it in the lower jaw and heavy enough to keep the fowl from flopping around too much. Figure 12 illustrates a very simple and economical way of killing for market; it is adapted to either scald or dry picking and is the method used by large commercial establishments.

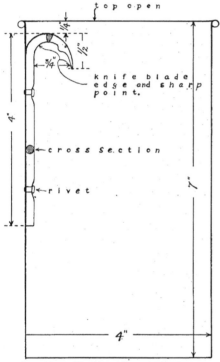

FIG. 11. Blood can for use in killing poultry.

FIG. 11a. Working plan of blood can.

Both hands are free to work with and there is no danger of the bird being bruised by flopping over the floor or against the wall after being stuck. The body feathers are put in the barrel. The wing and tail feathers may be thrown on the floor and swept up later or put in a small box at the side of the barrel. A small can of water can be hung from the side of the barrel by a hook if desired, to moisten the fingers when dry picking.

FIG. 12. Blood can being hooked into fleshy part of lower mandible to catch the blood after making the stick.

Fattening Crate.—In crate fattening the birds are shut up in crates each compartment of which is 3 feet long, 2 feet wide and 18 inches high. Sometimes they are made up in two compartment sections as shown in figures 13 and 13*a* or they may be made in much longer sections. The crates may be covered on all sides with lath or the lath may be used only in front with the other sides covered with 1-inch netting. The strips covering the front should be run vertically so that the fowls can poke their heads through and eat out of the trough in front. The strips are spaced 1½ inches to 1¾ inches apart for half grown fowls such as broilers and fryers, and 2 inches apart for mature fowls. Small market stock of the lighter breeds, such as broilers and small frys can often squeeze through strips 2 inches apart. While slats may be used for the bottom, ½-inch hardware cloth is much more sanitary and easy to keep clean and costs but a fraction more. The crates are usually placed two and three deep in the fattening house and a pan 1 inch deep and of the same size as the bottom of each compartment is placed directly underneath the bottom of every compartment to catch the droppings which fall through. These pans can be pulled out and cleaned every day without disturbing the birds. This arrangement keeps the coops clean and sanitary and the birds need not be

FIG. 13. Two compartment fattening crate complete.

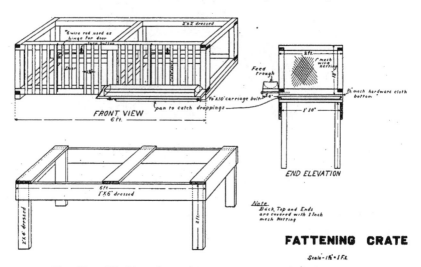

FIG. 13a. Working plans of two compartment fattening crate.

disturbed from the time they are put in till they are fat enough for market, the cleaning and feeding all being done from the outside.

The feed troughs can be made from ordinary 5-inch roll rim galvanized iron roof gutter cut to proper length and with ends soldered on. The local tinsmith will make such troughs at small cost.

Figure 13 illustrates a two-compartment, portable crate with feed troughs in position and one of the pans for catching the droppings partly pulled out. In figure 13a the methods of construction are shown in detail.

Supply Can.—Where a poultry raiser has a number of pens of fowls to feed and has to carry a big pail of grain from pen to pen, he is not only performing labor daily that could just as well be done once a week and with a wheelbarrow or horse and wagon, but at the same time

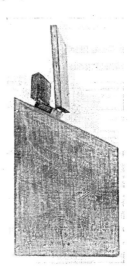

FIG. 14. Supply can for grain or mash. These views show two covers. The small cover at the rear was added to make it easier to pour feed out of the can as it is difficult to pour feed through the front cover on account of the slanting top. It may be made with either one or two covers as desired.

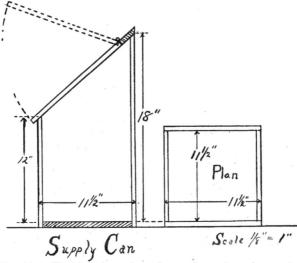

FIG. 14a. Working plans of supply can for grain or dry mash.

is wasting much valuable time unless he can gather the eggs and do the feeding on the same trip. However, where there are many eggs to gather it is usually necessary to make two trips; one to feed and one to gather eggs.

2—19325

By having in each pen a supply can large enough to hold a week's supply of grain for that pen and a dry mash hopper large enough to hold a week's supply of mash, the mash hoppers and supply cans need only be filled up once a week and the feed can be hauled in a wagon or cart. The poultryman can then walk from pen to pen each morning with his hands free for other things and scatter the right amount of grain to the fowls in each pen from the supply can in that pen. At night he takes his egg buckets, gathers his eggs and feeds as he goes along from pen to pen on the one trip.

Where each pen of fowls is large enough, bins may be built against the wall and arranged so that they can be filled from the outside. A galvanized iron or wooden barrel also makes a good supply can. The supply can illustrated in figure 14 may be made any size desired and has a slanting top that fowls can not perch upon. If not too large it can be hung on the wall out of the way. Where one would like to know the amount of feed eaten from week to week by any given pen or pens, the amount of feed put in supply can and hopper at the beginning of the week, let us say Monday morning after the morning feed, can be weighed in and the amount left at the end of the week (Monday morning after the morning feed) weighed back before weighing in a new supply. In this way accurate records of the feed consumption per pen or flock can be kept and also of the relative consumption of grain and mash.

Fig. 15. Hatching Egg Cabinet (modified Maine cabinet).

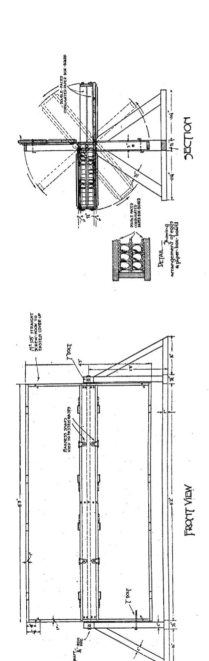

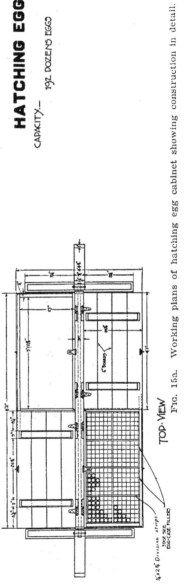

HATCHING EGG CABINET

CAPACITY:— 192 DOZENS EGGS   SCALE 1"=1'

Fig. 15a.   Working plans of hatching egg cabinet showing construction in detail.

Hatching Egg Cabinet.—In figure 15 is shown a labor-saving egg-turning cabinet for saving hatching eggs in. Where a great many eggs are set each season and they are all turned by hand, considerable time is required each day to turn them while they are being saved for the incubators. With the device illustrated, over 2,000 eggs can be turned at the same time by simply revolving the table on its axle. As can be seen from the illustrations, the table is divided into eight compartments with every compartment containing eight ordinary egg-case fillers, holding three dozen eggs each. Each compartment is again divided into 8 smaller sections by $\frac{1}{4}$ inch by $2\frac{1}{4}$ inch strips notched to fit together where they intersect (see drawing). Each of these small divisions holds one 3-dozen size egg-case filler. By having the table divided up in this way into unit sections of three dozen capacity it is very easy to keep eggs from special matings or special pens of breeders by themselves while being saved, a very convenient arrangement. Double faced corrugated card board is used to line the inside of the table and as partition walls between the upper and lower compartments. Ordinary harness snaps are used to fasten the covers when shut. Before turning the operator wants to be certain that every cover is firmly fastened.

Egg Sorting Table.—In sorting eggs, especially for incubation, it is often convenient to have a table on which the eggs may be sorted and on which they will stay where put without danger of rolling around or on the floor. The table shown in figures 16 and 17 is one that has been especially designed for this purpose. Persons who are doing trapnesting, pedigree breeding, keeping pen records of breeding stock as a substitute for trapnesting, will find such a table very useful in systematically arranging and recording eggs for the incubator.

Marking Eggs.—To clearly and easily identify hatching eggs from trapnested or pedigreed stock, a uniform system of marking should be adopted. As soon as the egg is removed from the nest it should be marked on large end with the hen number, pen number, date or any other information that is needed in identifying that particular egg. Example 281/7/3-24; hen number 281, pen 7, March 24.

In sorting these eggs for incubation, certain hen's eggs may be grouped into a separate incubator and the progeny toe marked when hatched, each hen's eggs may be set separately in pedigree trays and the offspring marked, or the eggs for each incubator may be arranged systematically on the sorting table in numerical order with each hen's eggs together and then transferred to the incubation record in the same uniform order. By thus recording the number of each hen's eggs set and the number of infertile, of dead germs at first and second test, dead in shell, and chicks hatched, a complete record is secured of the fertility and hatchability of the eggs of every breeding fowl in the flock. In the

FIG. 16. Egg Sorting Table. Note double top. The upper half of this double top is made in sections which slide in strips nailed to the lower part of table top. Only the upper sections have holes in them. The lower part is a solid smooth table top which is held firmly in place on the horses by cleats which fit closely into notched slideways on the horses.

FIG. 17. One corner of the egg room showing egg sorting table, egg scales and end of hatching egg cabinet.

same way by hatching the eggs from certain pens or groups of hens served by certain strong males in separate incubators, toe marking them when hatched and keeping mortality records by means of the toe marks, very efficient, yet easily secured pedigree records of the breeding flock may be kept and consistent improvement secured in the flock as a whole.

Egg Candler.—For candling market eggs or to test hatching eggs during incubation an electric candler is a great convenience. The one illustrated is not only very simple in design but permits of full use of all of the table top on which the work is being done. The candler is supported above the table on a verticle piece of pipe which also acts as a conduit for the electric wires. The holes in the bottom of the box throw plenty of light on the trays of eggs without in any way interfering with the operation of candling, another big advantage. A candler which throws light only through the one opening and leaves the trays or boxes of eggs in darkness, causes a waste of time in feeling around in the dark for the eggs and often results in a good deal of breakage.

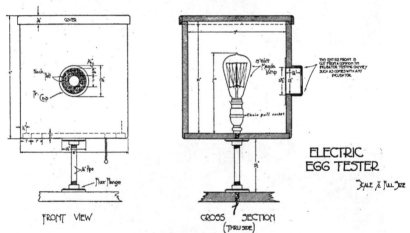

FIG. 18. Electric Egg Candler or Tester.

STATION PUBLICATIONS AVAILABLE FOR DISTRIBUTION.

REPORTS.

1897. Resistant Vines, their Selection, Adaptation, and Grafting. Appendix to Viticultural Report for 1896.
1902. Report of the Agricultural Experiment Station for 1898–1901.
1903. Report of the Agricultural Experiment Station for 1901–\3.
1904. Twenty-second Report of the Agricultural Experiment Station for 1903–04.
1914. Report of the College of Agriculture and the Agricultural Experiment Station, July, 1913–June, 1914.
1915. Report of the College of Agriculture and the Agricultural Experiment Station, July, 1914–June, 1915.

BULLETINS.

No.
168. Observations on Some Vine Diseases in Sonoma County.
169. Tolerance of the Sugar Beet for Alkali.
170. Studies in Grasshopper Control.
174. A New Wine-Cooling Machine.
178. Mosquito Control.
184. Report of the Plant Pathologist to July 1, 1906.
185. Report of Progress in Cereal Investigations.
195. The California Grape Root-worm.
197. Grape Culture in California; Improved Methods of Wine-making; Yeast from California Grapes.
198. The Grape Leaf-Hopper.
203. Report of the Plant Pathologist to July 1, 1909.
207. The Control of the Argentine Ant.
208. The Late Blight of Celery.
211. How to Increase the Yield of Wheat in California.
212. California White Wheats.
213. The Principles of Wine-making.
216. A Progress Report upon Soil and Climatic Factors Influencing the Composition of Wheat.
220. Dosage Tables.

No.
225. Tolerance of Eucalyptus for Alkali.
227. Grape Vinegar.
230. Enological Investigations.
234. Red Spiders and Mites of Citrus Trees.
241. Vine Pruning in California. Part I.
242. Humus in California Soils.
244. Utilization of Waste Oranges.
246. Vine Pruning in California. Part II.
248. The Economic Value of Pacific Coast Kelps.
249. Stock Poisoning Plants of California.
250. The Loquat.
251. Utilization of the Nitrogen and Organic Matter in Septic and Imhoff Tank Sludges.
252. Deterioration of Lumber.
253. Irrigation and Soil Conditions in the Sierra Nevada Foothills, California.
254. The Avocado in California.
255. The Citricola Scale.
256. The Value of Barley for Cows fed Alfalfa.
257. New Dosage Tables.
258. Mealy Bugs of Citrus Trees.
259. Commercial Fertilizers.
260. Availability Studies on Nitrogenous Fertilizers.

CIRCULARS.

No.
65. The California Insecticide Law.
69. The Extermination of Morning-Glory.
70. Observations on the Status of Corn Growing in California.
76. Hot Room Callusing.
79. List of Insecticide Dealers.
80. Boys' and Girls' Clubs.
82. The Common Ground Squirrels of California.
83. Potato Growing Clubs.
87. Alfalfa.
91. Disinfection on the Farm.
100. Pruning Frosted Citrus Trees.
101. Codling Moth Control in the Sacramento Valley.
106. Directions for using Anti-Hog Cholera Serum.
107. Spraying Walnut Trees for Blight and Aphis Control.
108. Grape Juice.
109. Community or Local Extension Work by the High School Agricultural Department.
110. Green Manuring in California.
111. The Use of Lime and Gypsum on California Soils.
113. Correspondence Courses in Agriculture.
114. Increasing the Duty of Water.
115. Grafting Vinifera Vineyards.
117. The Selection and Cost of a Small Pumping Plant.
118. The County Farm Bureau.

No.
119. Winery Directions.
121. Some Things the Prospective Settler Should Know.
122. The Management of Strawberry Soils in Pajaro Valley.
124. Alfalfa Silage for Fattening Steers.
125. Aphids on Grain and Cantaloupes.
126. Spraying for the Grape Leaf-Hopper.
127. House Fumigation.
128. Insecticide Formulas.
129. The Control of Citrus Insects.
130. Cabbage Growing in California.
131. Spraying for the Control of the Walnut Aphis.
132. When to Vaccinate against Hog Cholera.
133. The County Farm Adviser.
134. Control of Raisin Insects.
135. Official Tests of Dairy Cows.
136. Melilotus Indica as a Green Manure Crop in Southern California.
137. Wood Decay in Orchard Trees.
138. The Silo in California Agriculture.
139. The Generation of Hydrocyanic Acid Gas in Fumigation by Portable Machines.
140. The Practical Application of Improved Methods of Fermentation in California Wineries during 1913 and 1914.
141. Standard Insecticides and Fungicides versus Secret Preparations.

CPSIA information can be obtained
at www.ICGtesting.com
Printed in the USA
BVHW061639031218
534640BV00036B/3424/P